BE.

by Tabitha Mortiboy

SAMUEL FRENCH

FOR AMATEUR PRODUCTION ENQUIRIES

UNITED KINGDOM AND WORLD
EXCLUDING NORTH AMERICA
licensing@concordtheatricals.co.uk
020-7054-7298

Each title is subject to availability from Concord Theatricals,
depending upon country of performance.

USE OF COPYRIGHTED MUSIC

USE OF COPYRIGHTED THIRD-PARTY MATERIALS

IMPORTANT BILLING AND CREDIT REQUIREMENTS

BEACONS was commissioned by Attic Theatre Company and the play was first performed on 21st March 2016 at Park Theatre, London, directed by Philip Wilson, Set Designer Tom Rogers, Lighting Designer Matt Daw, Sound Designer Max Papenheim. The cast was as follows:

JULIE . . . . Tessa Peake-Jones
BERNARD . . . . Paul Kemp
SKYE . . . . Emily Burnett

BEACONS was performed on 14th July 2022 at Devonshire Park Theatre, Eastbourne Theatres, directed by Samuel Clemens. The cast was as follows:

JULIE . . . . Moira Brooker
BERNARD . . . . Steven Pinder
SKYE . . . . Polly Jordan

CREATIVE LIST
Writer – Tabitha Mortiboy
Director – Samuel Clemens
Original Design – Geoff Gilder and Andy Newell
Lighting Design – Douglas Morgan
Sound and Video Design – Sam Clemens
Production Manager – Ryan Tate
Deputy Stage Manager – Elliott Davis
Assistant Stage Manager – Sasha Louise Buckwell-Bailey

ACKNOWLEDGEMENTS
Beachy Head Chaplaincy Team
Tom Allen Media
Rebecca Fielding at Jordan Productions
Shelley Claridge
The Beachy Head Story

CAST

MOIRA BROOKER | JULIE
Moira trained at Bristol Old Vic School going on to perform leading roles at Manchester Royal Exchange, Young Vic and the Royal Court. She acted in and produced many new plays for New Vic Productions – often in partnership with Eastbourne Theatres, lastly in *Miss Dietrich Regrets*. Moira's extensive TV credits notably include Judith in BBC's *As Time Goes By*.

STEVEN PINDER | BERNARD
Steven has spent the past few years touring UK and Asia as The Wizard in hit musical *Wicked*. His vast theatre credits include: *The Memory of Water*, *Footloose* and an award-winning performance in UK tour *Dead Funny*. His most noted TV character is Max Farnham in Channel 4's soap *Brookside*.

POLLY JORDAN | SKYE
Polly trained at the Royal Central School of Speech and Drama. Credits include: *Trespass* (UK Tour); *Blithe Spirit* (Swansea Grand Theatre); *Black Roses* (Ribcaged Productions/Lancashire Theatre Workshop); *White Feather Boxer* (UK Tour); *Blood + Chocolate* (York Theatre Royal/Pilot Theatre); *I Walk In Your Words* (Tamasha Theatre/Rich Mix).

CREATIVES

SAMUEL CLEMENS | DIRECTOR

Samuel Clemens trained at the Drama Centre London and is an award-winning director of film, stage, audio drama and commercials. His extensive work includes films *Surgery* (multi-award winning), *A Bad Day to Propose* (Straight 8 winner 2021), *Say No* & *Dress Rehearsal*, plus audio dramas *Doctor Who*, *The Avengers*, *Thunderbirds*, *Stringray*, *Gallifrey* & *Callan* for Big Finish Productions & Anderson Entertainment.

Samuel directed new writing: *You Thought I Was Dead Didn't You?* at Waterloo East Theatre 2019, UK stage tour of *Strictly Murder* by his late father Brian Clemens OBE 2017, which he is currently making into a feature film.

Samuel's last piece of theatre before the pandemic was directing *Beacons* for Eastbourne Theatres in February 2020 and he is delighted to be back!

TABITHA MORTIBOY | WRITER

Tabitha is a writer based in London. Her latest production *The Amber Trap* ran at London's Theatre503, directed by Hannah Hauer-King and produced by Damsel. Her most recent theatre script *Daffy Grod and The Shaking Lights* was shortlisted for the Papatango Prize and longlisted for the Bruntwood Award. Her first play *Billy Through the Window* was shortlisted for the Brighton Fringe Excellence Award. In 2020 she was named runner up in the Alpine Fellowship Theatre Prize; in 2021 her script *Kissing Rice* was shortlisted for the inaugural Hope Playwriting Prize, and later that year her original seven-part audio drama *Life Sentence* was produced by Mags Creative and won the Gold Award at the ARIAS 2022 for Creative Innovation. *Beacons* was originally produced at The Park Theatre, London in 2016, where it picked up nominations for three Off West End Awards including Best New Play and Most Promising New Playwright. It first transferred to The Devonshire Park Theatre in March 2020 and is now returning for its second run.

DOUGLAS MORGAN | LIGHTING DESIGNER

Douglas's work as a lighting designer encompasses a wide range of productions, including musicals, plays, dance festivals and corporate work. National tours include: *She Stoops to Conquer, Travels With my Aunt* for Creative Cow; *Relatively Speaking, Nunsense, Dames at Sea, Deadly Game, Private Lives, Boogie Pete Live, By Jeeves, Gotta Sing Gotta Dance Tours, Last of the Summer Wine* for Eastbourne Theatres. Recent credits include: *Beacons, Return to the Forbidden Planet, The 39 Steps, One Man, Two Guvnors, Don't Dress for Dinner, Peter Pan, Round and Round the Garden, Summer Ice Spectacular* for Wild Rose Ltd; *The Quest* for New Vic Productions, *Stepping Out, Barnum, Neville's Island, Aladdin, Jack & the Beanstalk, Cinderella, Dick Whittington, Sleeping Beauty, Beauty and the Beast, Snow White, Robin Hood* all for Eastbourne Theatres.

EASTBOURNE THEATRES
CONGRESS · DEVONSHIRE PARK · WINTER GARDEN

Eastbourne Theatres comprises the Congress Theatre, Winter Garden and Devonshire Park Theatre. It is the largest Theatre complex on the south coast welcoming over 350,000 patrons each year.

Eastbourne Theatres take pride in its reputation as the premier producing house on the south-east coast, being the only local authority-owned theatre in the country to not only produce in-house but then also tour its own productions.

Eastbourne Theatres began producing in 2001 with a highly acclaimed production of Alan Ayckbourn's *Relatively Speaking*, starring John Challis and Sue Holderness. Subsequent productions have included: *Stepping Out, Taking Steps, You're Only Young Twice, Barnum, Nunsense, Dames at Sea, Neville's Island, By Jeeves, Gotta Sing Gotta Dance, One Man, Two Guvnors, Return to the Forbidden Planet* and *The 39 Steps*, many of which have toured nationally. The theatres have produced the annual Devonshire Park Theatre pantomime for the last 20 years.

As co-producers Eastbourne Theatres have worked with New Vic Productions on shows including: *Telstar* (Tour and West-End); *The Quiz* starring David Bradley (Tour and West-End;, national tours of *Blonde Poison, Miss Dietrich Regrets* and *Swimming at the Ritz*, as well as seasons of new work including several world premiere productions.

Other collaborators include; Original Theatre Company with *The Madness of George III, Twelfth Night, See How they Run, Wait until Dark* and *Night Must Fall*.

Eastbourne Theatres have even co-produced an *Ice Show* with sixteen international ice skaters and a cast of West End singers!

In 2020 Eastbourne Theatres first produced *Beacons* and are delighted this production is now returning to the Devonshire Park Theatre, a perfect homecoming for it being the venue is within such a short distance of the play's setting.

CHARACTERS

JULIE – (50s)
BERNARD – (50s)
SKYE – (16)

SETTING

Beachy Head, Eastbourne

AUTHOR'S NOTES

// indicates that someone takes a breath as if to interrupt the speaker.
/ indicates an actual interruption.

Beacons was the first play I ever wrote, and it is still the closest to my heart. It's a story about love and hope and human kindness. It's about resilience and magic and bravery and beauty. It's easy to lose sight of those things when the world feels threatened in so many ways, but they burn brightly even in the darkest moments. I hope the story of these three wonderful people reminds us all to be good to one another, to look for the light in the world, and to always eat ice cream x

For my parents, Sally and Steve.
You have always been my lighthouse: my constant guidance,
and my way back home.

Scene One

*(A low light rises on **SKYE**.)*

SKYE. There was a young man once. And he lived near here, near Beachy Head. He lived right down by Sovereign Harbour where the boats come in and the air tastes like the sea and smells a bit like fish and chips. And he fell in love with a girl. He used to say he fell for her hook, line and sinker. He was besotted. From the old English *sot*, to be drunk and silly. To be drunk on someone. He was drunk at the sight of her. He was devoted. And then, one day, years later, she left. And he climbed up here. And walked over the edge.

Or... or, sometimes, it goes like this –

(Quicker now.)

There was a young man once and he lived near here. He lived right down by Sovereign Harbour with the salty air and the fish and chips and he fell hook, line and sinker for this girl. This wild, untouchable, beautiful girl. And he was drunk on her, and giddy and happy and then one day she disappeared...

But he knows. He knows that she's out there somewhere. And every night he comes up here and stares across the water and pictures her in the distance. And he feels her, somehow, on the wind and in the air. And now, at night, as the summer gets colder, and the sky goes black and the sea goes black, something magical starts to happen. He closes his eyes, and this girl that vanished – she is suddenly beside him. And this piece of earth lights up like a dawn, and they dance together in this secret, honey-coloured light, and nobody asks how she's flown across the ocean. How she's flown in a moment over miles of water, stood softly beside him, and started to dance.

> *(The light spills outwards to reveal an ice-cream van and scattered tables.)*

BERNARD. I know how to dance.

SKYE. Go on then, let's see.

BERNARD. I learnt from a master of the Bavarian Waltz. Keep your chin up. And your back nice and straight, and keep exactly four inches between us.

SKYE. Exactly four inches?

BERNARD. Exactly. Four inches. Ready? Chin up. Chin up – one two three, one two three, that's how it goes, one two three, one two three, everyone knows /

SKYE. Hey Julie watch this!

BERNARD. Shh, she's counting, you know how she struggles.

JULIE. I heard that Bernard.

BERNARD. Did you? Good God, you've got ears like a bat.

JULIE. Well I've lost count now.

BERNARD. Surprise surprise.

JULIE. There's a mountain of coppers.

BERNARD. Do it later.

> *(He picks up a chocolate flake.)*

JULIE. I've a business to run, that's fifty p.

BERNARD. Fifty p?

SKYE. It's a pound, he's got two.

BERNARD. You bloody snitch.

(**SKYE** *has picked up a book of Beachy Head myths.*)

SKYE. Shh, I'm reading.

JULIE. This is why Kyle makes a bloody fortune. He's getting a brand new freezer and a brand new sign because he doesn't have two bickering babies by his van.

SKYE. And he's got an offer on his Mr Whippy's.

JULIE. Has he? What offer?

SKYE. Two for two fifty.

JULIE. Two for t – one for one twenty five?

SKYE. He'll have made a killing.

JULIE. One twenty five? They'll be the cheapest in Eastbourne.

BERNARD. They should be ninety nine p.

SKYE & JULIE. They're not ninety nine p.

BERNARD. Aren't they?

JULIE. No wonder we've got leftovers.

BERNARD. I thought they were ninety nine p.

SKYE. They're called ninety nine's because that's how you pour them.

> (*She swings into the van and pours herself an ice cream.*)

JULIE. You know that Kyle stole this pitch? I got here first and he skulked in later /

SKYE. You swirl it like that on top of the cone.

> (**SKYE** *goes for a flake –* **JULIE** *bats her away.*)

JULIE. 2003 I opened this van. In 2012, Kyle parks on the verge, a few hundred yards away, and starts pinching my customers.

SKYE. *(over.)* Pinching my customers.

(**SKYE** *lathers the ice cream in chocolate sauce.*)

JULIE. It's not funny Skye.

SKYE. *(With a mouthful of whippy.)* Well who changed the footpath?

JULIE. Kyle and his mob.

BERNARD. Well. The town council. But egged on by Kyle.

JULIE. This used to be busy, it used to be lively. I had hikers and trekkers non stop when I started.

BERNARD. Ey, it's exclusive, it's just off the beaten track.

JULIE. It's forgotten more like. Lay one new footpath, let mine grow over, let Kyle in with his big brash van /

SKYE. Why did they change it? What's wrong with the old one?

BERNARD. Because the sea is eating the earth.

JULIE. Because of coastal erosion. Every year we lose a bit of land and my van's getting closer and closer to the edge.

SKYE. *(With awe.)* Oh my God.

JULIE. *(In his general direction.)* So thank you Kyle you lump of lard.

(*She returns to the till.*)

He's an invader.

SKYE. An imposter.

BERNARD. A sodding interloper.

SKYE. Yeah, loping into this land of ours.

BERNARD. Though technically we're invaders Skye.

SKYE. We're not invaders!

JULIE. No you're part of the furniture.

BERNARD. Aren't you lucky.

SKYE. What, have you lived in Eastbourne your whole, whole life?

JULIE. Mm, hereabouts.

BERNARD. Her bones are made of chalk and clay.

JULIE. I'm not a fossil.

SKYE. *(To* **BERNARD.***)* Not like you.

JULIE. And I was once a bright young thing.

SKYE. I can't imagine when you were younger.

JULIE. What d'you mean?

SKYE. I just can't imagine a younger you.

JULIE. I was trendy back then. I was pretty back then. I had bell bottom jeans and hair down to my waist. And I was dating a boy called Fred Makardo.

SKYE. Fred Makardo?

BERNARD. Was he chubby and dull?

JULIE. No, he was gorgeous. Really gorgeous. And we had our first date at the bandstand in town and the band was playing Mr Bojangles and Fred was a fantastic dancer.

BERNARD. I bet he couldn't waltz.

JULIE. Oh he could do anything. He was a sea cadet. He married Mary, a mariner.

SKYE. *(Enjoying the sound.)* Married a mariner.

JULIE. He was very chivalrous. You don't get that nowadays.

BERNARD. I'm bloody chivalrous.

SKYE. When are you ever, ever chivalrous?

BERNARD. Right, last November, when the kettle was broken, I carried two cups of hot chocolate all the way up from town and I didn't even take a sip.

JULIE. No alright, that was nice, you're a good egg Bernard.

BERNARD. A good bloody egg?

JULIE. Yeah, salt of the earth.

BERNARD. Oh, a salty egg.

JULIE. Don't be grumpy.

SKYE. Humpty Dumpty.

> (**BERNARD** *scowls into his paper.*)

> (**SKYE** *nudges* **JULIE.**)

Shall we do our celebration?

JULIE. Oh God, I forgot! Yeah go on, get it out.

BERNARD. What celebration?

JULIE. You know damn well.

BERNARD. I don't want to celebrate.

> (**SKYE** *digs out a bottle of bubbly wine.*)

JULIE. Grab the big blue mugs.

SKYE. *(Pinching* **BERNARD**'s *cheek.)* The big blue mugs.

BERNARD. Cut it out.

SKYE. *(To* **JULIE.**) Right. You make a speech.

JULIE. Put the paper down.

BERNARD. I'm stuck on a clue.

SKYE. It's *The Water Babies*.

BERNARD. Y – how d'you know that?

SKYE. I did it already and rubbed it out.

BERNARD. You've done the whole crossword?

SKYE. Yeah it's easy that one.

BERNARD. You little bugger.

JULIE. Right, put it down.

SKYE. Can I open the bottle?

JULIE. You can but don't shake it.

> *(She turns to **BERNARD** as **SKYE** shakes the bottle.)*

Here's your cup and give us a smile.

> *(The bottle pops and covers **SKYE**.)*

> *(**JULIE** wipes down her face.)*

You silly sod.

BERNARD. I saw you shake it.

SKYE. *(In his accent.)* You bloody snitch.

JULIE. Right, now, give it here. Give us your mugs. Come on, on your feet. Right, OK. To a wonderful friend, and a wonderful man, who's finally got a home of his own. And here's to the glorious powers that be for finally putting your name on that list.

SKYE. To a room of one's own.

JULIE. To a brand new start.

SKYE. To a brand new chapter.

JULIE. And to the end of a wonderful summer. Cheers.

SKYE. Cheers.

BERNARD. OK. Cheers.

(The lights fall.)

Scene Two

(Two weeks later down at the van.)

(Most of the tables have been cleared away.)

(There is a sense of quiet, of Autumn setting in.)

*(**SKYE** sits on a bench with a ball of wool. It stretches back to **JULIE** who's knitting in the van.)*

(There's a laptop set to one side.)

SKYE. When you were little...

JULIE. Mm?

SKYE. Did you want to be an ice-cream lady?

JULIE. No.

SKYE. Did you want to be someone who saves lost souls?

JULIE. No I wanted to be an acrobat. I wanted to be an aerial dancer. You know with the silk that hangs from the ceiling.

SKYE. Is that why you like it up here? Up high?

JULIE. I don't know.

SKYE. It's unusual, you know, to be happy up high. Most people get queasy from vertigo.

JULIE. I'm a capricorn – I'm a mountain goat. We're sure footed and sturdy on rough terrain.

SKYE. Some people think it's 'subconscious desire'. They say vertigo isn't a fear of falling. It's not that you're afraid, it's that part of you wants to. And part of you wants to feel it, sort of like you're tempted.

JULIE. *(As if unconvinced.)* Hmm.

SKYE. Maybe it feels like flying.

JULIE. I don't think it feels like flying.

SKYE. No. We don't know.

JULIE. Here, give us more wool.

>   (**SKYE** *spools out the wool.*)

SKYE. What are you making?

JULIE. A jumper for Bernard. It's his birthday next month.

SKYE. *(Quietly, happily.)* No way.

JULIE. It's bloody hard work.

SKYE. Who taught you to knit?

JULIE. My mother. She was very good. She lost the knack towards the end, but she knitted me gloves when I was little. They're fiendish, gloves. Almost impossible.

SKYE. Can you teach me?

JULIE. You'd get restless.

>   (**SKYE** *smiles.*)

SKYE. Maybe.

>   *(They lapse into silence, the click of* **JULIE***'s needles tapping at the sea air.)*

I wanted to be a lighthouse keeper.

JULIE. Did you? You know they're automatic.

SKYE. Be nice up there. Dad says when it's clear you can see Paris from here. He said he once saw the Eiffel Tower. And he said he saw a woman on top feeding onions and macaroons to a poodle in a beret.

JULIE. Well he's got good eyesight.

...

    When are you off home?

SKYE. I don't know yet.

JULIE. Your mum must miss you. Your mum and dad.

SKYE. No, they're alright. They're away for a bit… dad's in the army.

JULIE. Is he?

SKYE. Yeah, I reckon I'm just gonna stay for a bit.

JULIE. How long for?

SKYE. I don't know yet. It's just quiet when they're away. It's just me at home.

JULIE. Course. It's just… well, it'll be even quieter now. I can't really afford /

SKYE. I know. I thought that.

JULIE. I'd love to have you /

SKYE. No, it's OK. I'm starting a new job.

JULIE. Are you? Where?

SKYE. At a dog grooming parlour down in town. It's called 'Pampered Pooch'.

JULIE. *(Over.)* Not Pampered Pooch? The one with the glitter?

SKYE. Yeah, and the feathers, she's mad that lady. My trial shift last week, this dog came in, it was half pug, half poodle, it looked like a cushion. They're called pug-a-poos, here look I'll show you /

    (She goes to the laptop.)

JULIE. No wait, wait a minute /

SKYE. What are you doing?

JULIE. No it's nothing.

SKYE. Julie what is it?

> (**JULIE** *takes the laptop.*)

JULIE. It's nothing. It's nothing /

SKYE. Give it back! Show me!

JULIE. Look, the thing is. And just, don't laugh.

SKYE. I won't. I won't laugh.

JULIE. It's. The thing is… I'm doing online dating.

SKYE. No. No way, can I have a look?

> (*She grabs the computer.*)

I like your picture.

JULIE. Oh God. Shut up.

SKYE. Julie McCarthy, Eastbourne, Sussex /

JULIE. No stop it, stop it.

SKYE. Alright OK sorry /

JULIE. Oh the internet's gone.

> (**JULIE** *takes the laptop and hovers it ahead of*
> *her – scanning the air as if to 'catch' the Wifi.*)

SKYE. Has it?

JULIE. Well done Skye.

SKYE. Me? What did I do?

JULIE. You knocked it out when you grabbed it like that.

SKYE. Knocked what out?

JULIE. The internet connection.

SKYE. You can't knock it out. What – what are you doing?

JULIE. It's over here somewhere, I caught it this morning.

(**SKYE** *takes a small device from her pocket and approaches* **JULIE**.)

SKYE. Here, try using this.

JULIE. What's that?

SKYE. It's a dongle. Give it here.

(**JULIE** *surrenders the laptop suspiciously.*)

JULIE. A what?

SKYE. It gives you the internet.

JULIE. It's a what?

SKYE. It's a dongle.

JULIE. A dongle.

SKYE. There you are.

JULIE. Oh right, OK.

SKYE. Right, let's have a look.

JULIE. Now, I've had a few – offers, from men on here. And I've narrowed it down to just these three.

SKYE. You're sneaky Julie /

JULIE. Stop it, be nice.

SKYE. I don't like this one.

JULIE. Why, what's wrong with him? He likes maple syrup, and rambling and badminton.

SKYE. He spelt badminton wrong.

JULIE. No, lay off.

SKYE. He's got a funny hairline.

JULIE. Has he? Where?

SKYE. There look, it's all scraggy.

JULIE. Oh. Maybe you're right.

SKYE. OK, who's the next one. Wentworth. Where's that?

JULIE. No that's his name.

SKYE. What Wentworth? Wentworth?

JULIE. Yes, that's a name /

SKYE. His name is Wentworth?

JULIE. Yes, that's his name /

SKYE. OK not him. So, last and least /

JULIE. Hey come on, be fair.

SKYE. No he's alright. Oh – wait, OK no.

JULIE. What's wrong with him?

SKYE. He's called Julian, Julie. You'd be Julie and Julian.

(**JULIE** *snaps shut the laptop.)*

JULIE. OK that's enough.

SKYE. No sorry, sorry. He does look alright.

JULIE. He is alright. We might meet up.

SKYE. Will you? When?

JULIE. I don't know, he's – he's better than nothing.

SKYE. You can do better than 'better than nothing'.

JULIE. Well I'm sick of sitting up here on my own.

SKYE. You're not on your own.

JULIE. You're shampooing poodles.

SKYE. I'll still come up. And there are customers here – and Bernard, sometimes.

JULIE. Bernard comes, I'll give you that. But customers come when the blue moon rises.

SKYE. Since the weather?

JULIE. Since the summer stopped.

SKYE. How's Bernard been?

JULIE. He's been busy I think. He's moved into his flat.

SKYE. Has he? Already?

JULIE. So it is just me really. It's just me and Mr Whippy.

SKYE. You should do more coffees.

JULIE. I do do coffees.

SKYE. Yeah, but the thing is…

JULIE. What?

SKYE. Well the thing is that Kyle's got a coffee machine. He does cappuccinos and lattes and things.

JULIE. Oh bloody hell. J – bloody hell.

(She turns to her knitting with extra force.)

SKYE. Are you working later? Tonight I mean?

JULIE. Why?

SKYE. When d'you start?

JULIE. Why?

SKYE. Do you think I could come?

JULIE. No Skye, I've told you.

SKYE. I won't say a word, I wanna see what you do.

JULIE. We just keep an eye out.

SKYE. Yeah /

JULIE. And we walk around for five hours on a bloody cold cliff edge.

SKYE. So, I love a good walk.

JULIE. You're not trained.

SKYE. Trained in what?

JULIE. In talking to people.

SKYE. I can talk.

JULIE. You can talk. Yes. You can certainly talk /

SKYE. So trained in what?

JULIE. You know what, Skye, it's different /

SKYE. I don't see how /

JULIE. No I don't s'pose you do. But it's different. It's different.

SKYE. Why is it a secret?

JULIE. It's not a secret.

SKYE. What if I met somebody? What would I say?

JULIE. You wouldn't, you'd phone us, that's what we're here for // and that's what we're trained in. So try not to worry.

SKYE. You could train me.

JULIE. It takes months, Skye.

SKYE. Well give me the short version.

JULIE. Skye.

SKYE. Please.

JULIE. No.

SKYE. Please.

JULIE. No. Not now. Chin up… hey, chin up.

                ...

SKYE. Do you ever think you've missed the obvious man?

JULIE. No, I don't, who's the obvious man?

SKYE. The man who is totally smitten with you. Who bought you hot chocolate last November / and didn't even take a sip.

JULIE. No. No. You can pack that in.

SKYE. Why? He's clever and he's nice when he's not being moody /

JULIE. I said pack it in. He's a very good friend.

SKYE. Is it because he was homeless before? / Because he's not anymore, he's an eligible bachelor.

JULIE. No! Of course not, don't be so silly. He's a friend, though, a friend, and that is that.

SKYE. Well he's nice. He's nicer than Wentworth and Julian and "badgemington" man.

JULIE. Stop it.

SKYE. Fine. But /

JULIE. Stop it.

SKYE. Fine.

> (**JULIE** *keeps knitting.*)

> (*A light beam rises, then fades away.*)

JULIE. There goes the lighthouse.

SKYE. There she goes.

JULIE. Do you really think you'd like it up in that tower?

SKYE. Yeah. It'd be cosy. You'd be calling people home.

JULIE. You're an old romantic.

SKYE. It's true.

JULIE. I s'pose.

SKYE. And you'd be out at sea. In a floating cottage.

JULIE. You're obsessed with that water.

SKYE. Because it's big. And mystic. And it's got secrets inside it.

JULIE. Has it? What secrets?

SKYE. I don't know. Messages in bottles. And sunken ships.

...

I looked up what you said about the van. About how the land's disappearing now. And you know there's a town in Suffolk – there's this whole old town that fell into the water. And it had this church, it was called All Saints, and it's all under water now. The steeple and the huge steel bells and the aisle and everything. At the bottom of the ocean.

...

It's pitch black at the bottom, did you know that? There is absolutely no light. It's just thick, inky, sticky black.

JULIE. Bloody hell Skye, your head.

SKYE. But imagine that. And imagine the tides under water that can move whole boulders and slabs of rock. It's like the ocean's got muscle. It's like it's alive.

JULIE. Well. It's scary if you stop and think. So we just push on. Pig headed and cheerful.

(She tugs back the wool.)

Here, pass that back. I give up on this, we've been here for hours.

SKYE. Not much business today.

JULIE. No. They're fair weather friends. Welcome to the seaside.

(The lighthouse beam pulses gently as the lights sink.)

Scene Three

(A few days later.)

*(**JULIE** is pulling down the shutters when **BERNARD** enters.)*

BERNARD. Hello hello.

JULIE. *(With quiet delight.)* Bernard.

BERNARD. You closing up?

JULIE. It's been drizzling all day, I've had enough.

BERNARD. I've got an umbrella.

JULIE. You're going up in the world.

BERNARD. I'll be prime minister next.

JULIE. God help us. Sit down if you like, I'll do you a coffee.

BERNARD. Kyle's doing cappuccinos /

JULIE. Yes. I know.

BERNARD. I don't like cappuccinos.

JULIE. No, fluffy milk. Waste of money.

BERNARD. Has Skye gone back home?

JULIE. No, she came by the the other day.

BERNARD. I thought she was only here for the summer.

JULIE. So did I, but she's working in town now. She got a job at Pampered Pooch.

BERNARD. No.

JULIE. I know.

BERNARD. Bloody hell.

JULIE. She likes to keep busy.

BERNARD. She'll have college won't she? This time of year?

JULIE. She didn't say.

BERNARD. Her folks don't mind?

JULIE. No they're abroad. Her dad's in the army.

BERNARD. Is he? Oh right.

JULIE. How's the new flat?

BERNARD. Bit lonely.

JULIE. You hated the crowd in that hostel before.

BERNARD. I know but it's different just me on me own. I'm rattling around.

JULIE. Have you made it nice?

BERNARD. No, not really. I've not got pictures or photos and things. I've got a few books I put up on a shelf and it's got its own kettle so that's alright.

JULIE. Are you eating alright?

BERNARD. Yes thank you mother.

JULIE. I mean not out of tins.

BERNARD. There's nothing wrong with spaghetti hoops.

JULIE. We've had this discussion.

BERNARD. And I wasn't persuaded.

JULIE. I'm doing a lasagne later. I'll bring you a batch tomorrow.

    ...

Your shoes are squeaking.

BERNARD. Well then I shall have music wherever I go.

(She reaches for the shoe.)

JULIE. You need new boots Bernard, these are older than I am.

(He passes it over.)

BERNARD. I like these boots.

JULIE. They're falling apart.

BERNARD. They're very well loved.

JULIE. There's fresh socks in the bag.

(She patches up the shoe as **BERNARD** *searches for the socks. Instead he draws a patterned woollen hat from the bag.)*

BERNARD. Fancy number.

JULIE. I've been practising with colours.

BERNARD. Oh right. What d'you think?

JULIE. Ooh, you look gorgeous.

(He finds another hat and a colourful scarf.)

BERNARD. Bloody hell you've been busy.

JULIE. I've got time on my hands.

(He dons the scarf.)

BERNARD. How about now?

JULIE. Heart stopping.

BERNARD. They'd look better on you. Mind you everything does.

JULIE. Aren't you charming.

BERNARD. Well. I do try.

*(***JULIE** *hands back the shoe.)*

JULIE. Here hold that on tightly. The glue's still drying.

...

BERNARD. Are you busy later?

JULIE. I'm working again.

BERNARD. Are you busy tomorrow? Tomorrow evening?

JULIE. No they'll need me again. They're short on numbers.

BERNARD. Right. OK. You're a real life angel.

JULIE. I thought you didn't believe in angels.

BERNARD. No, not the kind with golden wings. Or silly little harps or chubby bums. But people like you. I think you're angelic.

JULIE. No, nonsense.

BERNARD. You're the kindest person I know.

JULIE. Then you need to meet more people.

BERNARD. Well, as it happens, I have made a friend.

JULIE. Have you?

BERNARD. Well, a neighbour.

JULIE. What are they like?

BERNARD. She's old. She's eighty. She's a fortune teller.

JULIE. Oh right, I see.

BERNARD. She gave me a reading the other day.

JULIE. What did she see?

BERNARD. Well it was a bit, y'know – impromptu. In that she didn't have a crystal ball or a mug of tea leaves or anything like that. But she stopped me, you see, on my way upstairs, and she beckoned me down to crouch on the floor. And she was totally silent, and she got out a hanky and she polished away at this old brass door knob.

JULIE. And you were just sat there?

BERNARD. Well, I was intrigued.

JULIE. Right. Go on.

BERNARD. She polished away till it was properly shiny and then she looked into it, like a crystal ball.

JULIE. Only it was a doorknob.

BERNARD. And she stared at me, and I said "what can you see?"

JULIE. You didn't believe her?

BERNARD. No, I was intrigued.

JULIE. And what did she say?

BERNARD. She said, "I see two things, very clearly. The first," she said... "it will rain tomorrow".

JULIE. When was this?

BERNARD. This was Tuesday just gone, and / it did rain on Wednesday.

JULIE. *(Over.)* Oh it did rain on Wednesday.

BERNARD. Exactly. It did. Which makes me think she knows what she's doing.

JULIE. So what was it then? Her other prediction?

BERNARD. Well, she went very still. And she held her breath. And she said "Everything. Is about to change." She said to get ready.

JULIE. Get ready for what?

BERNARD. For everything changing.

JULIE. That's not a prediction.

BERNARD. Well, we'll have to see.

JULIE. She sounds like a con artist.

BERNARD. I didn't bloody pay her.

JULIE. No I should hope not. You've not got two pennies to rub together you can't be paying old ladies to look into doorknobs.

BERNARD. That sounds a bit suspect.

JULIE. What looking through doorknobs with elderly ladies?

BERNARD. Like a peeping Tom.

JULIE. With a fetish for copper.

BERNARD. It takes all sorts.

JULIE. I know, believe me.

BERNARD. How do you know?

JULIE. No, I don't know.

BERNARD. No, come on, own up. What d'you know about all sorts?

JULIE. Nothing. Nothing. Liquorice All Sorts.

BERNARD. Come on, spit it out.

          …

    What?

JULIE. … I've been going online.

BERNARD. Online? What for?

JULIE. For – online dating.

          (His smile fades.)

BERNARD. Dating? What for?

JULIE. I'm bored of my own company, I don't know. It's just an experiment.

BERNARD. You're not on your own.

JULIE. I am most of the time.

BERNARD. Well, I'm here aren't I?

JULIE. Oh don't be so serious. It's a load of nonsense. I've had all sorts of pictures I never asked for and all sorts of messages, there's no proper filter.

BERNARD. Well then stop it, you plonker.

JULIE. It's a bit of fun. I delete all the riff raff /

BERNARD. Do you? What's left?

JULIE. It's just something to do, it's silly, it's nothing.

BERNARD. Online dating. It doesn't sound right. Not up here, not with that out there, those miles of water. It doesn't fit. It's prosaic. It's stupid.

JULIE. Yeah, all right Bernard, it's just a beach, and a bench and a bloody ice-cream van. It's not made of magic /

BERNARD. I know that /

JULIE. So just – leave it.

      (Rain starts to fall.)

Perfect.

BERNARD. Sorry.

JULIE. I know, I know. It's been a long day.

      *(**BERNARD** raises his brolly.)*

BERNARD. Here, come under here.

JULIE. Sorry. Sorry. I'm tired, that's all.

BERNARD. It's alright.

      ...

Perhaps we'll see a rainbow.

JULIE. Course we won't, the sun's gone in.

BERNARD. I don't know. It's shining somewhere.

      (The lights fall.)

Scene Four

(The next day.)

(SKYE holds wool as JULIE knits.)

(She tugs it taut and JULIE looks up.)

(A wollen tug of war ensues.)

SKYE. You said yes?

JULIE. I'm intrigued.

SKYE. I can't believe you said yes.

JULIE. He might be nice.

SKYE. He might be dreadful.

JULIE. *(To taunt.)* He might be sexy.

SKYE. He looked proper weird.

JULIE. I've said yes now.

SKYE. Do you know about 'badgemington'?

JULIE. No. I can ask.

SKYE. That'll be fun.

JULIE. Look it's your fault really.

SKYE. Me? Why's it my fault?

JULIE. You gave me that dongle, you kept me online. I'd have stayed cut off. I'd have surrendered to your wilderness and your bleak sea air.

SKYE. Maybe you should've.

JULIE. He might be nice.

SKYE. When are you going?

JULIE. ...any time now.

*(**SKYE** tugs tighter and **JULIE** stops knitting.)*

SKYE. Any time now?

JULIE. What's wrong with that?

SKYE. You never said.

JULIE. Well he drives this way, he'll have just finished work.

SKYE. What about me?

JULIE. You've locked up before.

SKYE. Yeah, but...

JULIE. What?

SKYE. You never said.

JULIE. I'm telling you now.

SKYE. You're being weird.

JULIE. No I'm not.

SKYE. Yes you are. You're being all shifty.

JULIE. I'm not shifty.

SKYE. You are. You're running away.

JULIE. He's picking me up.

SKYE. Well I was going to ask you out.

JULIE. You what?

SKYE. For a walk or something. Later.

JULIE. You were not.

SKYE. I was! I was actually.

*(**JULIE** pulls on her coat.)*

What time are you back? We can do something later.

JULIE. I'm working again.

SKYE. Again? How come?

JULIE. It's a funny time of year.

SKYE. Is it? What d'you mean?

JULIE. It's getting colder. Autumn's setting in.

SKYE. Does it make a difference?

JULIE. Sometimes. Some years.

SKYE. So the Autumn and the Winter – they make it worse?

JULIE. It's not – they can do.

> (**JULIE** *turns to gather her things.*)

SKYE. *(Quietly.)* The fall.

JULIE. What?

SKYE. They call it the fall. In America, don't they?

JULIE. Don't say that.

SKYE. It's weird, that's all.

JULIE. You can lock up early if it starts to rain.

SKYE. Can I come with you later? I can come back when it's time.

JULIE. No Skye, come on.

SKYE. I don't see why not.

JULIE. I've told you why not.

SKYE. I'm bored on my own.

JULIE. Go down to the bandstand.

>   …

What's the matter?

SKYE. Nothing. Nothing's the matter.

...

JULIE. When do you start college?

SKYE. Not for a while.

JULIE. Not now? Not September?

SKYE. No. Not for a while.

(**JULIE***'s phone beeps.*)

Is that him?

JULIE. How do I look?

SKYE. Nice. You look lovely.

JULIE. Hey. Chin up.

SKYE. This doesn't feel right. It's not right you leaving.

JULIE. I can't stay here forever.

SKYE. Well be careful.

JULIE. Course I will.

SKYE. And phone me. If he's weird. I'll keep it on loud.

JULIE. I'll be fine.

SKYE. I can't believe it.

JULIE. Wish me luck.

SKYE. Good luck. Good luck.

(**JULIE** *exits.*)

(**SKYE** *looks on as she leaves.*)

(*She's alone at the edge for a moment.*)

(*She returns to the van, hops inside, and sets to work experimenting with ice-cream concoctions.*)

*(After a moment, **BERNARD** enters. To begin with, **SKYE** is obscured from his view.)*

BERNARD. Hello hello.

SKYE. Hiya Bernard.

BERNARD. Skye. Where's Julie?

SKYE. She had an appointment.

BERNARD. Oh right. Shall we have a cuppa?

SKYE. Yeah.

(She swallows a spoonful of chocolate sauce.)

Yeah, sorry.

*(**BERNARD** digs into his coat pockets and produces a book or two from each.)*

BERNARD. Here, I brought you some more books.

*(**SKYE** takes the small stack.)*

SKYE. Thanks.

BERNARD. A selection of my favourites. And there's some poems in there, you should learn some by rote.

SKYE. *(Over.)* By rote. I know. Thanks.

BERNARD. It's good for the brain. Not to mention the mind.

SKYE. *(Over.)* 'Mention the mind' – I know. I will.

BERNARD. What's up ey?

SKYE. Nothing. Nothing's up.

BERNARD. Go on.

SKYE. It's nothing.

BERNARD. How's the new job?

SKYE. How's the new flat?

BERNARD. It's OK.

SKYE. Me too.

BERNARD. We're both growing up.

SKYE. I know. Is that good?

BERNARD. I dunno. God knows.

SKYE. It's making us pensive.

BERNARD. Is it? Good word.

SKYE. It's my word of the day. I've done them all week. Pensive. Wretched. Morose. Monotone.

BERNARD. Cheerful.

SKYE. I'm reading a thesaurus. It's actually good.

BERNARD. A thesaurus? Bloody hell.

SKYE. Don't be rude. Or –

(She struggles to pronounce it.)

Contumelious.

BERNARD. What does that mean?

SKYE. It means being rude.

BERNARD. You've a good vocabulary.

SKYE. It's inexhaustible. Unrelenting. Unremitting. Long. Extensive.

BERNARD. Otherwise known as bafflegab. Or logorrhoea.

SKYE. What does that mean?

BERNARD. It just means verbal diarrhoea.

SKYE. Bugger off Bernard.

BERNARD. Another good word.

SKYE. Bugger. Bastard.

BERNARD. Bombastic baboon.

SKYE. Bombastic. You win.

BERNARD. Derived from where?

SKYE. From the Latin bombax – which meant cotton or padding. To bombast, which means words that sound clever when really they're nonsense, like cotton stuffed words. To bombastic which means pretentious and silly and full of hot air.

BERNARD. Good. Very good. Now, about your outfit.

SKYE. What's wrong with my outfit?

BERNARD. It's just – quite yellow.

SKYE. It's my only mac.

BERNARD. It's not very trendy.

> *(She picks up a Cornetto and hurls it at his head.)*

Oi.

SKYE. It's my dad's.

BERNARD. Oh. Right, sorry.

SKYE. And you can't talk.

BERNARD. Me? I'm just rugged.

> *(He throws her a bag of sweets.)*

Here, have a fruit pastel.

SKYE. They're all green.

BERNARD. I don't like that flavour. I got them in a care pack from the local school. They get the kids to make them in a harvest festival.

SKYE. We used to do that. We used to send tins of beans and tomatoes to all the old ladies.

BERNARD. Yeah well it's patronising.

SKYE. No it's nice.

BERNARD. Well I got them and a copy of *Beano*. And a pair of sunglasses. Silly little bugger.

SKYE. It's the thought that counts.

BERNARD. Course it's not, I could've done with a jumper. Or a new pair of shoes.

SKYE. Dad used to give them spaghetti hoops. I'd go in to school with ten big tins of spaghetti hoops and nothing else. He says he reckons they're good for the soul. But mum says that's stupid and the sauce tastes like paint.

BERNARD. Your dad sounds like a bloody sensible bloke.

SKYE. Yeah. I s'pose.

     ...

BERNARD. So what's this appointment? Where's she gone?

     ...

SKYE. She's gone on a date.

BERNARD. You what?

SKYE. On a date.

BERNARD. On a date with who?

SKYE. I don't know really.

BERNARD. Well what did she say?

SKYE. They met online.

BERNARD. Who is he?

SKYE. I don't know.

BERNARD. Well where did they go?

SKYE. I don't know Bernard.

BERNARD. Did you see him?

SKYE. No.

BERNARD. Was she excited? Had she dressed up nicely?

SKYE. I dunno. A bit. He picked her up.

BERNARD. From here? He came here?

SKYE. No, down at the road.

BERNARD. In a car?

SKYE. Yeah. I s'pose.

        ...

BERNARD. Bloody hell.

SKYE. I know.

        ...

I always thought you might ask her.

        (There is silence as **BERNARD** *absorbs this.)*

        *(***SKYE** *watches him.)*

Dad was in love with my mum for ages. And then one day they were walking home from college and he plucked up the courage and he held her hand. And then they got married and had me. It's easy really.

        ...

BERNARD. Julie says your dad's in the army.

SKYE. Yeah.

BERNARD. You must miss them.

SKYE. Yeah. I s'pose.

BERNARD. Where are they now?

SKYE. Ages away. Shall we play a game?

BERNARD. No.

SKYE. Let's play pictionary.

BERNARD. No.

SKYE. Right I'll go first.

BERNARD. I don't like this game.

SKYE. You never try properly.

BERNARD. I always try.

SKYE. Why are you so grumpy?

BERNARD. Why are you so tetchy?

SKYE. I'm not t – just play.

BERNARD. Go on then I'm waiting.

SKYE. Y – right then come on.

> *(She starts to sketch on the whiteboard by the van.)*

BERNARD. And nice and big, I've not got me glasses.

SKYE. You don't have any glasses.

BERNARD. Exactly.

SKYE. Take it seriously.

BERNARD. This'll be fun.

> *(He watches her sketch.)*

Debbie Harry.

SKYE. What?

BERNARD. Boris Johnson.

SKYE. Come on.

BERNARD. The dustbin monster.

SKYE. It's a palm tree Bernard.

BERNARD. Why d'you tell me?

SKYE. You're rubbish at this.

BERNARD. You're bloody impatient.

SKYE. Right let's play the tightrope.

> *(She goes towards the bench, hops onto its back and walks slowly across it, her arms outstretched.)*

BERNARD. Right that's not fair.

SKYE. Oh nothing's fair.

BERNARD. I'm just – I'm top heavy. I always fall off.

SKYE. Here's a little known fact about the canine species. The fatter they are, and the shorter they are, the better they are at bodily balance.

BERNARD. How d'you know that?

SKYE. I work at the dog parlour.

BERNARD. You're making it up.

SKYE. No I promise, it's true.

BERNARD. And I'm not a dog.

SKYE. Well, same idea.

BERNARD. And I never said fat, that's your word madam.

SKYE. Madam?

BERNARD. I'm not fat.

SKYE. I'll bet you a pound I can get right across it four times in a row.

BERNARD. I don't have a pound.

SKYE. Yes you do, you fat liar.

BERNARD. Right, come on then.

> (**SKYE** *starts across but soon topples and falls.*)
>
> (**BERNARD** *catches her and spins about.*)

You owe me a pound.

SKYE. Alright put me down. Put me down, put me down!

> (*He sets her back on the arm of the bench.*)
>
> (*She wobbles again and reaches for his shoulder.*)

It's windy that's all.

BERNARD. Ey, don't blame the wind.

SKYE. Fine, double or nothing.

> (*The lights lower and music begins* * *– it gradually swallows their voices.*)

BERNARD. Shut up, get down.

SKYE. You're just jealous you're not athletic.

BERNARD. I was athletic, back in the day.

SKYE. Oh back in the day.

BERNARD. Don't be cheeky young lady.

SKYE. God you're such an old man. Come on, double or nothing. Double or nothing.

> (*The lights come down.*)

---

* A licence to produce BEACONS does not include a performance licence for any third-party or copyrighted music. Licensees should create an original composition or use music in the public domain. For further information, please see Music Use Note on page iii.

Scene Five

(The next day.)

(JULIE, SKYE and BERNARD are sitting at the van.)

(BERNARD is wearing his sunglasses and flicking idly through the Beano.*)*

(SKYE has her nose buried in a new book of myths.)

(JULIE is knitting.)

(They speak over each other as they squabble.)

JULIE. He's just built a pond with his own bare hands.

BERNARD. How manly.

JULIE. And he's got thirteen Japanese carp and a beautiful garden apparently / with –

SKYE. People put lipstick on Japanese carp.

JULIE. What?

SKYE. People dress them in make up.

JULIE. I don't think that's true.

BERNARD. They're a symbol of luck /

SKYE. It is true /

BERNARD. Why did he buy thirteen? /

SKYE. And earrings and tiaras and stuff.

BERNARD. Bloody hell.

JULIE. That's not true.

BERNARD. He sounds right bloody odd.

JULIE. It's not true.

BERNARD. Dolling up goldfish.

JULIE. He doesn't – forget it.

(She goes back to her knitting.)

(They go back to their reading.)

He's just got a greyhound.

SKYE. Where from?

BERNARD. A greyhound?

JULIE. I don't know – what's wrong with a greyhound?

BERNARD. They're not proper dogs.

SKYE. Well he should've got a rescue, they kill them when they're old.

JULIE. Yes they are – no they don't.

SKYE. It's true. I read it.

BERNARD. They're dead scrawny and odd.

JULIE. No they're not.

SKYE. What's it called?

JULIE. Well he'd only just got her, and he hadn't named her yet. So he's naming her after me.

SKYE. Julie?

BERNARD. No.

SKYE. That's a bit weird.

JULIE. Why?

BERNARD. Because it's a dog.

JULIE. Would y – what's wrong with you two?

SKYE & BERNARD. Nothing.

JULIE. You're sulking.

SKYE. No.

BERNARD. *(Over.)* No I'm not.

          ...

JULIE. Who wants a cup of tea?

SKYE. Yeah I do.

BERNARD. Yeah go on.

          (**JULIE** *stands to put the kettle on.*)

SKYE. Is he good looking?

BERNARD. Is he?

JULIE. I don't know.

SKYE. What's he like? Did he look like his photo?

JULIE. I don't know.

BERNARD. When did you see a photo?

SKYE. Last week.

JULIE. Not really. He's very tall.

BERNARD. Let me see a photo.

SKYE. It's on the computer.

BERNARD. Well where's the computer?

JULIE. He's got little glasses. And a little moustache.

BERNARD. He's got a moustache?

JULIE. But he's friendly. So.

BERNARD. He sounds like a bastard.

JULIE. We've run out of sugar.

SKYE. Kyle's got some.

(JULIE pauses, expecting SKYE to go.)

(She sighs, exasperated.)

JULIE. Right. Right I'll go.

(She exits.)

(SKYE and BERNARD watch her leave.)

(They turn back to their books.)

BERNARD. *(Grumbled into the* Beano.*)* You never told me you'd seen his photo.

SKYE. Have you heard about the monk in black?

BERNARD. Oh ay, the ghost that stalks the edges.

SKYE. Do you think it's true?

BERNARD. Um. No not really.

SKYE. Makes sense though.

BERNARD. Does it?

SKYE. If King Henry shut down all the monasteries. If he sacked all the abbots and chased them all away. And if it's true what they say and they shackled this monk and threw him over the cliff edge. It makes sense he'd be angry.

BERNARD. Yeah, that part makes sense.

SKYE. And then. If he's angry. He could tempt people out. His ghost or his spirit could lure people over.

BERNARD. OK. What for?

SKYE. 'To take revenge on the living'.

(BERNARD raises an eyebrow.)

That's what it says here.

BERNARD. Oh it must be true.

SKYE. Everyone says it. There's something out there.

BERNARD. Not everyone says it. Those books might say it. But they are bombastic.

(*She half turns to her book.*)

SKYE. There's a satellite shower tonight. Can we go? Are you busy?

BERNARD. No.

SKYE. Do you know how many stars there are?

BERNARD. No I've never counted.

SKYE. Guess.

BERNARD. One or two.

SKYE. Five hundred. Thousand. Million.

BERNARD. Oh right.

SKYE. And that's just in the Milky Way.

BERNARD. Right.

SKYE. There are seventy thousand million million million in the whole wide world.

BERNARD. Is that right?

SKYE. I think so. Why, what is it really?

BERNARD. I don't know.

SKYE. Yes you do. You know everything really.

(**SKYE** *puts down her book and picks up another.*)

(*She casts* **BERNARD** *a look and tilts her chair towards him, trying to coax him out of a moody silence.*)

This one's about the Armada. I found it down the library.

BERNARD. Oh right.

SKYE. Do you know about the bonfires?

BERNARD. Mm.

SKYE. Imagine that. All up the coast these enormous fires to warn each other. In the dead of night, people stood round the flames as the ships get closer. Huddled together and scared witless – and seeing other fires light up miles away – like someone's heard what you've said. 'Cause they were messages, weren't they? Like a call to arms. Like a chain of whispers right up the coastline.

BERNARD. Mm. Imagine.

(**SKYE** *scowls at his disinterest.*)

SKYE. You love this stuff.

BERNARD. Sorry.

SKYE. I know why you're moody.

BERNARD. Do you Miss Marple?

SKYE. You need to tell her.

BERNARD. Tell who?

SKYE. You know who.

BERNARD. Tell her what?

SKYE. You know what.

BERNARD. ...shut up.

SKYE. Tell her. I dare you.

(*The lights fall.*)

Scene Six

(Late that night.)

*(**SKYE** enters with binoculars slung around her neck.)*

*(**BERNARD** follows, stops, and peers upwards through his own binoculars.)*

BERNARD. Ah well. Not to worry.

SKYE. It's not fair Bernard. They said we'd see a satellite shower. I don't even know what that looks like. I was picturing fireworks and shooting stars with their tails fizzing and burning and exploding.

BERNARD. Oh well, you would've been disappointed anyway then.

SKYE. I wanted to see it at least. And it's all going on.

(She peers through the binoculars.)

It's all happening behind that cloudy curtain.

BERNARD. You're a little poet.

*(**SKYE** casts a look to **BERNARD**, then begins a passage learnt 'by rote'.)*

SKYE. "And we are here as on a darkling plain. Swept with confused..."

BERNARD. "Alarms"

SKYE. "Alarms of struggle and flight. Where ignorant armies clash by night"

BERNARD. *(Over.)* "Clash by night"

*(**BERNARD** chuckles.)*

SKYE. Julie says it's just a beach. She says I'm always too romantic.

BERNARD. Well. There's a certain feeling up here.

SKYE. You said there wasn't. You said it was nonsense that stuff in my book.

BERNARD. No, not monks in black that tempt you over. Not all that hokey pokey stuff. There's just a feeling.

> …

Don't look at me like that.

> …

SKYE. Do you want a ninety nine? I've got the keys. I've got provisions in here as well.

> *(She unzips her rucksack and lines up a picnic.)*

I've got hot chocolate, and marshmallows and extra whippy whipping cream.

BERNARD. You don't pack lightly.

SKYE. Dad says if you're gonna do a picnic, you have to take it seriously. Never just a sandwich and a packet of crisps. You need a wicker basket and a proper blanket, and a punnet of strawberries and a flask of tea. Only I don't have a blanket or a basket or a punnet. But I do make the best ninety nines in Eastbourne.

> *(As she turns to pour the ice creams, **BERNARD** picks up the whipped cream.)*

> *(He glances surreptitiously at **SKYE**, then tilts his head back, covers his face in cream and creeps towards the hatch.)*

You're the first to try my brand new recipe. I've invented a special called the Big Blue Sky /

BERNARD. Oh look the moon's come out.

> (**SKYE** *turns.*)

Boo!

> (*She stumbles backwards in shock.*)

You look like you've seen a ghost.

> (*She slings a handful of sprinkles towards his face.*)

SKYE. You scared me Bernard!

BERNARD. I'm the man in the moon.

> (*She picks up a bottle and squirts it towards him.*)

SKYE. Have some strawberry sauce.

BERNARD. Ow! That's right in me eye.

> (*She pours it into her mouth.*)

SKYE. It's delicious this flavour.

BERNARD. I'm a Sheffield Mess.

SKYE. You've distracted me Bernard.

BERNARD. Oh sorry, crack on.

> (*He wipes his face and licks the sauce.*)

SKYE. In the Big Blue Sky there is blueberry sauce –

BERNARD. Oh you're right that is nice.

SKYE. And white marshmallows and coconut sprinkles.

BERNARD. That sounds a bit much.

SKYE. It's a maverick concoction with perfect results.

BERNARD. Right then let's have it.

SKYE. The finishing touches –

(She adds the sprinkles.)

– there. Try that.

BERNARD. Doesn't look great.

SKYE. No but it will. It's a work in progress.

BERNARD. Bloody hell that's not bad.

SKYE. See. I could do it. I could be an ice-cream lady.

(She peers through the binoculars towards the clouds.)

BERNARD. Or you could go back to college and learn something proper.

(He follows her gaze.)

There's a gap in the clouds.

SKYE. If we wait we might see it.

BERNARD. It's worth a try.

SKYE. Let's play a game.

BERNARD. No.

SKYE. Come on I've got a good one. Right, how you play. You imagine you're doing online dating /

BERNARD. No.

SKYE. You imagine you're doing online dating and we have to write a profile. So I have to pick four words for you. And you have to pick four words for me.

BERNARD. No that's not a game /

SKYE. No but it's fun. Right we've got five seconds /

BERNARD. Five seconds?

SKYE. In three, two, one.

...

Right. You in four words. You are hairy, northern, kind but cross.

BERNARD. Northern?

SKYE. I only had five seconds.

BERNARD. That's racist.

SKYE. No it isn't.

BERNARD. We'll you're little and irritating and I dunno, annoying.

SKYE. That's two, one's a synonym.

BERNARD. Is it? Oh well.

> *(She reaches for the flask of hot chocolate and takes a mug from her bag.)*

SKYE. Right, this is part two of the Big Blue Sky. It's a winter warmer. Here, pass that here. Trust me. Trust me, give it here.

> *(She upends his ice cream into the mug.)*

BERNARD. What are you doing?

SKYE. Wait and see.

> *(She covers it in hot chocolate and whipping cream and passes it back.)*

BERNARD. What've you done?

SKYE. Try it and see. It's a work in progress.

BERNARD. Oh this one and all?

SKYE. Yes. They're experiments. No one rushed Einstein to discover – anything.

BERNARD. No. Fair point.

SKYE. Let's play another game.

BERNARD. No not now Albert.

SKYE. I do this one with dad. You close your eyes, and you put your heads together, and you count to three. And you open them up and you whisper 'owl eyes' and it looks like a huge, enormous bird.

BERNARD. Why would you do that?

SKYE. Because we're waiting for the stars Bernard. We could be here for ages.

BERNARD. Bloody hell.

SKYE. Ready? Come over here. Come on, come over here.

BERNARD. You're unusual aren't you?

SKYE. Now put your head here. And close your eyes. Ready?

> ...

One, two, three. Owl eyes! – See. It's good.

> ...

What?

BERNARD. Do you speak to your dad?

SKYE. What?

BERNARD. Can you phone him where he is?

SKYE. Yeah, I can phone him.

BERNARD. And your mum?

SKYE. Yeah, why?

BERNARD. Well, maybe you should.

SKYE. Well, yeah, I do.

BERNARD. My dad was in the army. I know it's not easy.

SKYE. Yeah but it's fine.

BERNARD. What unit's he in?

SKYE. I can never remember.

BERNARD. Well, don't lose touch.

SKYE. I'm alright on my own.

BERNARD. I know, but they're important your mum and dad.

SKYE. I know that Bernard. Why are you being serious?

BERNARD. No. Sorry… it's just I never really bothered. I never wrote when my dad was away. And then, when he died I wished I had. I'm not, I'm not saying /

SKYE. No. No it's OK.

BERNARD. Sorry. I do seem to say the wrong thing.

SKYE. It's OK.

BERNARD. I just mean I regret it. So give 'em a bell.

SKYE. Yeah. OK.

> …

I always forget that grown ups have a mum and a dad.

BERNARD. It's easily done.

SKYE. Where's your mum?

BERNARD. Oh. Long gone.

> (**SKYE** *watches him closely.*)

SKYE. So you're an orphan.

BERNARD. Well. I'm in good company. Oliver Twist. Annie. Little Nell. Bambi.

> (**SKYE** *laughs quietly.*)

Ey I didn't mean you should be nervous – I'm sure your dad's fine.

SKYE. Yeah, no, I know.

BERNARD. They're probably having a lovely time. Sunbathing and all sorts.

SKYE. Yeah probably.

(He peers through his binoculars towards the sky.)

Do you think it's over?

BERNARD. I don't know.

...

SKYE. Bernard?

BERNARD. Mm?

SKYE. Have you ever come up here with Julie? When she comes here in the evenings?

BERNARD. No.

SKYE. She won't let me. She won't even tell me what they do, not properly. She just goes off sometimes in her funny outfit and her walkie talkie. She says they wander up and down.

BERNARD. They probably do.

SKYE. And save lost souls.

BERNARD. Something like that.

SKYE. Have you ever seen it?

BERNARD. What?

SKYE. Someone out here.

BERNARD. No.

SKYE. I get dizzy when I go too close to the edge.

BERNARD. Stay back then.

SKYE. They say there's an urge if you go out too far.

BERNARD. Not this again.

SKYE. No, no, not a person. Not a ghost. Just, like, a tugging. Like something's tugging you.

BERNARD. Don't be stupid.

SKYE. It's true.

BERNARD. It's not true at all.

SKYE. You said there's a feeling.

BERNARD. I meant it's – atmospheric, or – beautiful, maybe, I didn't mean bloody magnetic forces.

SKYE. There are people who've fallen because of the wind. And the mist, it gets misty. It can get so misty you can hardly see one foot in front of the other.

BERNARD. I know.

SKYE. You know a few years ago, in December, it was fifty two miles an hour the wind... imagine that.

BERNARD. How d'you know that?

(She shrugs.)

SKYE. Reading.

BERNARD. Right.

SKYE. And then there are girls who've thrown themselves off and been caught on the air in their huge white dresses.

BERNARD. Pack it in.

...

SKYE. When it happens. If it's not an accident. Then do you think it's romantic? Or at least a bit brave?

BERNARD. No I think you're being stupid.

SKYE. Why?

BERNARD. Because it's never about that. It never about being bloody brave. It's about real people who die up here.

> ...

SKYE. I didn't know about the cliffs before. I didn't know what people do.

> ...

When I was younger we came here on a summer holiday. But I can only remember the beach and fish and chips and the bandstand and the arcade. And I went paddling with dad while mum went swimming. She always goes out as far as she can and sort of disappears. She's not afraid of the water.

(She looks to **BERNARD** *and smiles.)*

I know where there's a better view.

(She goes to the van and climbs onto its roof.)

BERNARD. What are you doing?

SKYE. Don't tell Julie.

BERNARD. Get down.

SKYE. It's amazing up here.

BERNARD. Go on, get down.

(She looks towards the sky.)

SKYE. See those stars at the edge, those three in a line? That's me, and you and Julie. We're a constellation.

(She lowers her gaze.)

And there it is. I can see the sea.

(She catches her breath.)

Dad's got this video at home. And it's him and my mum and they're both loads younger. And they're down at the beach, and it's really sunny. And mum looks quite like me, it's weird actually. And she's laughing, they both are, like big, proper belly laughs and she looks so happy. And dad's got the camera, and then he turns it around and it's both of them, and he goes "tell the camera" and she's all shy and she looks down but dad's beaming. Like – properly beaming. And then she puts her head on his shoulder. And it's weird 'cause it fits exactly there. Like a little sunny, sandy puzzle with mum and dad and their massive smiles. And he goes "tell the camera" and she won't, but she's smiling. And then dad looks at the camera, and he's crying, and he says "we're having a baby". And they're talking about me. It's the day they found out about me. And it looks like everything... is perfect.

(The lights fall.)

Scene Seven

(Late that night.)

*(**SKYE** is alone now.)*

(She stands on the verge in a thin t-shirt, buffeted by the heavy winds and soaked by the sound of distant waves.)

(Behind her, in dim light, her coat and jumper are strewn across the bench.)

(A torch beam scans the cliffs.)

*(**JULIE** walks slowly forward.)*

JULIE. Skye. What are you doing?

...

Come here love. Come over here.

...

Come on love you'll freeze out here.

...

Skye /

SKYE. I want to feel it.

JULIE. Come on, come back.

SKYE. No I just. I just want to feel it.

JULIE. What's going on Skye?

...

Come and sit down and tell me what's happened... or don't. Or don't, you don't have to tell me.

...

Will you come and sit down?

SKYE. The wind gets stronger doesn't it? The closer you get to the sea. I went right out and I could feel it.

...

And when I touched the edge... if you brush your hand across, it's true... it sort of crumbles.

> (**JULIE** *picks up* **SKYE***'s coat and holds it towards her.*)

JULIE. Put this on.

...

SKYE. Can I tell you something?

JULIE. Of course.

SKYE. Please don't be angry.

JULIE. *(Quietly.)* No.

SKYE. I came this summer because I wanted to find you.

JULIE. OK.

SKYE. I wanted to meet you. I don't really know why.

JULIE. OK.

SKYE. But... I think that you knew my dad.

...

He's not in the army. He was a gardener actually. And his hands were always muddy.

...

And. Um. He's quite tall. And he's got scruffy hair, and it's black, it's dark black and he's got green eyes. And he's strong, you can tell it to look at him. You know, he's got big, broad shoulders.

    …

And he came… here… on New Year's Eve. Do you remember?

    (**JULIE** *catches her breath.*)

And the next day you phoned my house. But no-one was at home. Do you remember?

    …

Do you remember?

JULIE. Why didn't you tell me?

SKYE. And then you phoned again. And again, and again, you left all these messages in my old house.

JULIE. I had no idea.

SKYE. I heard it from you. From your voice on this machine. On my own in a hallway on this fucking machine.

JULIE. You were on your own.

SKYE. Yes I'm on my own, I am on my own.

    (**JULIE** *reaches towards her.* **SKYE** *shrugs her off.*)

You were offering to pray for us. You said "can we pray for you and your family". And I remember because that was the day I stopped having a family… you never told me that you pray.

JULIE. It's – the team does that, the people I work with. We work with the church /

SKYE. Did you? Did you pray for me?

JULIE. Yes.

SKYE. Why?

JULIE. In case it helped.

> ...

SKYE. What did you say? When you found him here?

JULIE. Skye, please / don't do this...

SKYE. Can you please tell me what he said? Did he mention me? Did he say he had a daughter?

> ...

Did he talk about my mum?

JULIE. No.

SKYE. I know that's why he came. I know he was frightened.

JULIE. ...what happened?

SKYE. ...she left us both. She just left last summer and I know that he needed her, I know that's why he came.

JULIE. Where is she?

SKYE. I don't know. I don't know.

JULIE. You should have told me Skye.

SKYE. Told you what? Told you what? That my mum got restless and ran away? That makes me sound useless.

JULIE. You should have told me that your dad /

SKYE. You were here, you were with him.

JULIE. No, I wasn't... nearby /

SKYE. But you spoke to him /

JULIE. No /

SKYE. You said that's what you do. When you come here at night you said you talk people down, you've been trained, you told me /

JULIE. I didn't have time.

SKYE. What do you mean?

JULIE. I wasn't close enough.

SKYE. You were with him. You said, you were with him that night /

JULIE. I was here, but far off /

SKYE. But you could have held him. If you were here you could have held onto him /

JULIE. I wasn't close enough Skye /

SKYE. And he would have held on, I know he would because he didn't let go of things. Even after mum left and he stopped speaking and listening, he still held on if I held his hand.

     ...

Where were you?

JULIE. I was back by the road.

     (**SKYE** *watches her, waiting.*)

I'd finished my shift and I was driving home. And I saw him. From a distance. And I stopped and I got out, and I did go towards him. And he turned around. And he started coming towards me. It was... I think he thought I was somebody else. And then he realised I wasn't. I wasn't whoever he'd hoped for. And he started going backwards, much quicker than me. He was running, almost, and I couldn't keep up.

SKYE. Did he fall? Did he slip? Because the wind out here // it's as fast as a car, it can knock you over, I've read that it can. It can push you like a person and the mist – if it's misty you can't see a thing, he could have tripped or, or stumbled. It does happen. It happens.

     (**JULIE** *nods but can't put her right.*)

You could have run to him /

JULIE. I tried.

SKYE. You could have run faster /

JULIE. I couldn't, I couldn't /

SKYE. You could, you could have stopped him and I could still have a dad /

JULIE. I couldn't, Skye it happened too quickly /

SKYE. I could still have a dad and he'd be at home now and the house would be warm /

JULIE. I'm sorry /

SKYE. And instead I live here in a fucking hostel and I have to sit in a room and remember that I wasn't enough. That my mum disappeared and I wasn't enough /

JULIE. You can't think like that /

SKYE. *(Exploding.)* That is all I can think!

        ...

JULIE. Nobody understands /

SKYE. Your job, your job is to understand, I came to find you to understand.

JULIE. I'm sorry, I don't. I don't understand.

SKYE. Was he frightened? I mean did he look frightened?

JULIE. No.

SKYE. I hate the thought that he was frightened. Or that anything hurt or broke /

JULIE. Stop. Stop it.

SKYE. Because Bernard shouts at me when I read those books. And you tell me I'm stupid for thinking it's magic, or for thinking there's something... slightly... better. But if there isn't... if it's really just the edge, and then the drop, and then endless cold water – if that's all there is then there is nothing left. He's just a sinking body – that used to be really strong and that used to carry me and hug me and squeeze my hand – but he's not just a body. Do you understand? It's not just a body it's my dad, he's my dad, and he's out there – somewhere.

...

JULIE. It doesn't mean he didn't love you. You know that, don't you?

SKYE. It means he loved mum more.

JULIE. No /

SKYE. It's OK. I knew.

...

When I was little I crept out of bed once and sat on the stairs and I could see mum and dad, I could see them in the kitchen. And mum was at the window, and dad was watching her. And he was just... amazed.

...

Bernard looks at you like that.

JULIE. No /

SKYE. He does / he does but you won't let him /

JULIE. He doesn't Skye, and Bernard /

SKYE. But you should /

JULIE. Bernard is not your dad.

...

(SKYE *looks away – musters her courage.*)

SKYE. You know how at night – it's not just the sun going down. It's not just the sky changing colour, it's this quiet, shimmering sort of thing... do you think that's like dying? It doesn't mean you stop existing, so there must be another side to it. And I think... I think dad's just on the other side of something. And I think he's found mum, and that they come up here, when everyone else is asleep, and they dance together in this patch of sun that I can't see. But they're together. Because they should be together. Even if it means that I'm here on my own. Or with you. And with Bernard.

...

I'm sorry I lied. And I'm sorry I stayed – that I stayed for so long. But I can't... I don't want to go home.

(*JULIE is still for a moment.*)

(*She goes suddenly to* SKYE *and hugs her tightly.*)

JULIE. I am so glad you came. I am so – I am so glad you came.

Scene Eight

(The next morning at the van.)

*(***BERNARD*** fusses over a bunch of flowers that he's set on a table.)*

*(***JULIE*** enters.)*

JULIE. Bernard.

BERNARD. Hello… you look tired.

JULIE. I am tired.

BERNARD. What's happened?

JULIE. What are these?

BERNARD. They're for you. They're for you because I wanted to talk to you.

> …

Would that be OK? I'll be quick.

*(***JULIE*** is still.)*

(She seems to know what's coming, but she doesn't have the will or the words to stop it.)

The thing is – we joke, don't we? I'm always saying you look gorgeous as if it's a joke and we're larking about. But – well…

*(***JULIE*** goes to speak.)*

No. Hang on a minute. I want to say this now I've started.

> …

When I say that you're gorgeous, there's... there's never been a time when I haven't meant it. And you... you're this ray of sun. I feel lucky to be near you /

JULIE. Bernard /

BERNARD. I'm sorry, I know. I know I sound bonkers. And I know I'm not exactly eligible. But I want you to know... don't marry this other bloke.

JULIE. I just met him.

BERNARD. You know what I mean.

> ...

Don't make me say it. I've never said it. I've never heard it said, not in my direction.

> ...

OK.

> ...

I love you. And I can scrub up quite nicely.

> ...

What d'you reckon? Eh?

JULIE. You're my best friend Bernard /

BERNARD. I could make you happy /

JULIE. You do make me happy /

BERNARD. Then give us a chance /

JULIE. No. Bernard. No.

BERNARD. Why not?

JULIE. Because that's not what this is. Let's not mistake what this is.

> ...

BERNARD. Can I tell you what I think this is?

JULIE. Bernard /

BERNARD. I think you're too comfortable being on the outside. Because for so long you've been up here on the edge and you've been on your own and life – life has gone on around you. And you've served families ice cream and young couples coffee and it's just been you inside that van. And you went to that church after your mum died because it was somewhere to go. And you joined that group that patrols up here // not just for something to do. You did it because you were so used to looking after people and I think you come here every night because it's exactly what you're used to. And you've made the mistake of thinking that I – that I am just like every other person you've helped, and then let go of. And you won't let me in.

> *(As if exposed,* **JULIE** *speaks now with a kind of aggression.)*

JULIE. Why do you think you love me?

BERNARD. I don't think. I do.

JULIE. Then why? Why do you love me? You love me because of what happened when we met. This is not a normal love affair /

BERNARD. It doesn't matter what happened when we met. I'm not just a patient. I will always thank you for what you did. I would have done it, if it hadn't been for you. If you hadn't stopped me I would have done it. And that's – you must never stop. Because for every person who dies up here there's another person you save /

JULIE. I don't save /

BERNARD. I know you don't like that word. I know you think it's heroic and romantic and silly but it's true. Every person you find and you talk to and you stop is a person you save. That's a life that you've saved.

And I was – grateful is just not big enough. But I was grateful. And then I got to know you. Because you let me. Because you were good enough to let me know you. And then, only then... I started to love you. Not out of gratitude. But just as any man might love any woman. And I know I've been homeless. And I know all I've got now is a tiny measly flat with a fortune telling neighbour, but I do, I do love you. And you should be loved. You are not just a lifeguard. You deserve to be loved in a normal, huge, whole hearted way. And as for that man you found on the internet. You cannot love a man who names a dog after you.

...

Just give us a go. And chuck me if you think I'm a nuisance.

JULIE. I can't.

BERNARD. Skye reckons it's a good idea. She put me up to it.

JULIE. Because she's scared of what will happen if you don't.

...

BERNARD. What?

...

JULIE. You wonder why I think I'm on the outside. But even Skye, even when I dare to think I've found someone who just likes being here – and I have loved her company, as pathetic as that sounds – even then when I think I've found a normal... someone, who's got nothing to do with that bloody cliff edge.

...

She's here because I saw her dad walk over the edge. Last new year when I was driving home.

BERNARD. Last new year? I remember, you were –

JULIE. Terrified. I was terrified. I didn't work at night for weeks /

BERNARD. I know /

JULIE. But I didn't tell you – properly.

(*This comes as an admission.*)

Skye came to find me because I phoned her house when he died... I found his number and I phoned what I thought was his family house because I had no idea that Skye, who was sixteen, who was a child, was there on her own. I phoned – and that is so unethical and stupid and against the rules and obsessive and selfish. I phoned for me. I phoned to get that image out of my head, of this man, this young man walking over the edge. I have never been so close and I have never seen the look on someone's face and I could not forget it. So yes, you're right, for every person that lives there's a person who dies up here. And Skye's dad died, it was him that night.

BERNARD. How long have you known?

JULIE. She told me last night when I was up here again for another bloody patrol.

BERNARD. Where is she now?

JULIE. She's at work. She's at work because she can carry the entire world on her shoulders and then get up every morning and smile.

...

And she's so happy.

(*She half laughs in disbelief.*)

She's always been so happy.

...

BERNARD. What did she want? When she came to find you?

JULIE. I don't know, an explanation. Some comfort, some sense, some idea of why her dad had just died.

BERNARD. What did you tell her?

JULIE. That I don't understand. And that I couldn't stop him and that I'm a huge, horrible disappointment. But she still wants to stay because there's nowhere else to go.

BERNARD. She can stay, she should stay, of course she can stay /

JULIE. She can't Bernard because she's all muddled up. She only wants to stay because she doesn't know what else to do /

BERNARD. It doesn't matter why /

JULIE. She's confused.

BERNARD. She's not stupid.

...

You're at it again. You don't believe for a second that you're important. You're daft not to have noticed but she think you're fantastic.

JULIE. It's misguided. She just needs somebody, I'm a substitute.

BERNARD. What's wrong with that? I don't think that's true but if it were there's nothing wrong with that.

JULIE. If it's not true then what's happened? Why is she still here?

BERNARD. What's happened is that she came here in need of a friend and she found one. And you're too stubborn to realise it's you. Just like you're too stubborn to realise I'm besotted and not just because, once upon a time, you saved my life.

> …

Julie, she needs you. And I need you // but not just as someone to lean on. Not as a counsellor or a chaplain but as a friend or as a… more than a friend.

JULIE. I can't Bernard because if we fight or fall out /

BERNARD. I'll not jump. You have to let me be a little bit more than the man you found who nearly jumped. And I'd like you to be happy. You've spent your life making other people better, it's high bloody time that you were happy.

> *(They watch each other.)*

Can I kiss you?

> …

Can I give you a hug?

> *(They hold onto each other.)*

> *(The lights fall.)*

Scene Nine

(That evening.)

(JULIE sits by the van.)

(SKYE approaches with a bunch of flowers.)

JULIE. Hello.

SKYE. Hello.

(She spots BERNARD's flowers.)

(Smiling.) What happened?

JULIE. It was your idea.

SKYE. Did it work?

JULIE. It might've done.

SKYE. Mine aren't as fancy.

JULIE. They're lovely.

SKYE. They're for you.

JULIE. Are you OK?

SKYE. Does Bernard know?

(JULIE nods.)

JULIE. Is that OK?

(SKYE nods.)

Can I do anything?

SKYE. Can we go back to normal?

(JULIE nods and begins to put out the flowers.)

JULIE. Did you pass the bandstand?

SKYE. It's busy already.

JULIE. They're the best band in Eastbourne.

      ...

SKYE. You'll never guess who I saw on the way.

JULIE. Who?

SKYE. That man from online with his new pet greyhound.

JULIE. No.

SKYE. I'm sure it was him with his funny moustache.

JULIE. He stood me up yesterday.

SKYE. Yesterday?

JULIE. We were supposed to have a drink.

SKYE. You never said.

JULIE. He said he forgot. He said he'd been with Julie at a puppy training class.

SKYE. No way.

JULIE. Good riddance. He did have naff hair, you were right about that.

      ...

SKYE. Are we alright?

JULIE. Course we are.

      (**BERNARD** *approaches.*)

      (**JULIE** *nudges* **SKYE.**)

He's wearing his jumper. I couldn't wait.

      (**BERNARD** *comes into view in a badly knitted, bright blue jumper.*)

BERNARD. One cup of sugar, courtesy of Kyle.

　　　…

　　Hello love.

SKYE. Hi Bernard.

　　(He smiles gently.)

　　I like your jumper.

BERNARD. Thank you. Kyle says it matches my eyes. Here, he's got another offer on his Mr Whippy's.

JULIE. No.

SKYE. How much?

BERNARD. A cone for a quid.

JULIE. A pound?

SKYE. No way.

　　(A song in the style of [MR BOJANGLES]* *– floats up from the bandstand.* SKYE *turns.)*

　　They've started.

　　(She climbs onto the van for a better view.)

　　*(*JULIE *stops still at the sound of the song.)*

JULIE. *(Quietly.)* No.

BERNARD. I arranged for them to play it.

JULIE. You didn't.

---

* A licence to produce BEACONS does not include a performance licence for "MR BOJANGLES". The publisher and author suggest that the licensee contact PRS to ascertain the music publisher and contact such music publisher to license or acquire permission for performance of the song. If a licence or permission is unattainable for "MR BOJANGLES"X, the licensee may not use the song in BEACONS but should create an original composition in a similar style or use a similar song in the public domain. For further information, please see Music Use Note on page iii.

BERNARD. Whatever it takes to trump Fred Makardo.

SKYE. He's being chivalrous.

> *(***JULIE*** *turns to* **SKYE**.*)*

JULIE. Get – Skye! Get down.

SKYE. I can see the beach.

BERNARD. Can you see the Eiffel Tower?

JULIE. You'll break our van.

SKYE. Whose van?

JULIE. Our van.

BERNARD. Do you fancy a dance?

JULIE. I've not danced for years.

SKYE. He learnt from a master of the Bavarian Waltz.

BERNARD. It's true. And as it goes – I'm fantastic.

> *(They begin to dance as* **SKYE** *looks out towards the bandstand.)*
>
> *(She turns back to watch them as the lights lower, and a pool of sunlight grows around the van.)*

The End

Lightning Source UK Ltd.
Milton Keynes UK
UKHW021814140722
405868UK00010B/963